Creative Patchwork

June Field, a keen patchwork collector, is a regular contributor to the *Financial Times*, the *Daily Telegraph*, *Collector's Guide* and *Antique Finder*, on collecting, and style and colour in the home. She also works as fashion and colour adviser for an internationally known home decoration group.

Front cover illustration by courtesy of American Folk Art,
73 Sloane Avenue London S.W.3

Hexagon patchwork.
Printed cottons 1837. (*Victoria and Albert Museum, London*)

Creative Patchwork

An Introduction to Patchwork and Quilting

JUNE FIELD FRSA

Also available in this series
Crochet Emily Wildman
Candlemaking Mary Carey
Jewellery Thomas Gentille
Macramé Mary Walker Phillips
Rugmaking Nell Znamierowski
Weaving Nell Znamierowski
Bargello Geraldine Cosentino
Filography Douglas K. Dix
Home Decoration Isabel Hunt
Country Crafts Valerie Janitch
Children's Clothes Jill Morris
Gifts Pamela Rodway
Appliqué Evangeline Shears & Diantha Fielding
Furniture Making John Trigg & David Field
Soft Toys Mabs Tyler
More Soft Toys Mabs Tyler
The Art of Dried and Pressed Flowers
   Pamela Westland & Paula Critchley
The Art of Shellcraft Paula Critchley
Pottery Tony Birks
Leatherwork Anne & Jane Cope
Picture Framing Anne & Jane Cope
Machine Knitting Hazel Ratcliffe
Papier Mâché Peter Rush
Good Housekeeping: Home Dressmaking

First published 1974 by Sir Isaac Pitman and Sons Ltd
This edition published 1976 by Pan Books Ltd,
Cavaye Place, London SW10 9PG
3rd printing 1982
© June Field 1974
ISBN 0 330 24795 6
Printed in Great Britain by Cripplegate Printing Co. Ltd., Edenbridge

Contents

Acknowledgements

My deep appreciation and thanks to Joan Field (no relation), who read through the book, and to the numerous patchworkers who have provided instructions on how to make their beautiful work. Without them this book could not have been written. Also to the National Federation of Women's Institutes (in particular Valerie Duthoit); *Home and Country* magazine; Sanderson (particularly the team who helped stage the exhibition – Clive Blunt, Ann McKimm, Sally Reeve-Tucker, Christine Whitehead, Richard Bett and his staff at Uxbridge).

For help and expert advice given on the basic methods of producing patchwork I am indebted to Michael Melia of Jem Patchwork Templates, and Dorothy Weir and her daughter Heather Ashcroft.

For inspiration and background knowledge of patchwork I read the excellent books of Averil Colby, Anne Dyer, Doris Marston, Alice Timmins, and many others.

My thanks also, for the excellent photographs taken by: Millar & Harris; Focus 4; *Worksop Guardian*; *Radio Times* Hulton Picture Library.

Sorting patchwork ready for judging. Betty Showler, Joan Field and Dorothy Crampton, National Federation of Women's Institutes judges, with Richard Bett of Sanderson of Reed International.

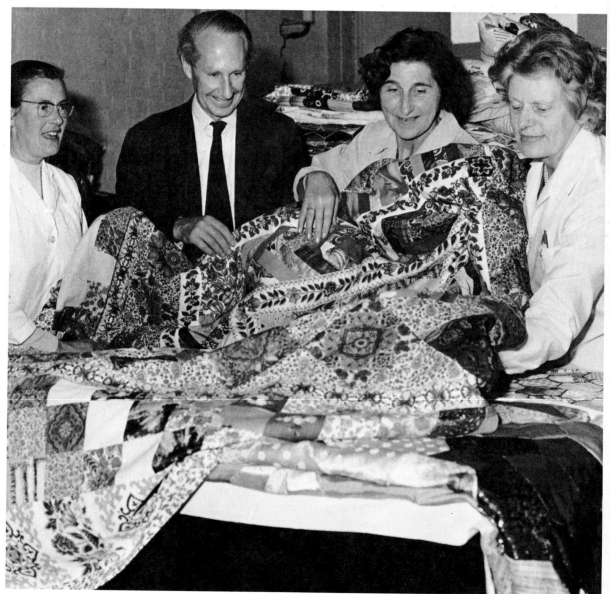

Preface

I first became interested in collecting and learning more about patchwork when I organized a competition and exhibition of patchwork for the National Federation of Women's Institutes* at Sanderson House in London in the early 1970s. None of us thought that this fascinating, yet basically simple country craft would come to life in such magnitude – yet the exhibition displayed over eight hundred items, three hundred and fifty of them quilts, and at least half of them quite old and extremely fragile, with the rest of the work made up of numerous small things ranging from bell-pulls to bikinis, bonnets to boxes, handbags to hot water bottle covers – all in patchwork.

'It began to dawn upon me that I might be buried under an avalanche of quilts', wrote a bemused American woman in the early 1900s after she had arranged a patchwork quilt show at a small county fair, and I know just how she felt! Her bright idea was so successful that it brought in quilts by the dozen. After an hour she sent a general alarm to friends and kindred for help . . . 'by some magic of desperation we got those quilts on display, one hundred and eighteen of them, by one o'clock'. So records Marie D Webster in *Quilts : Their Story and How To Make Them*.

A fair amount of the magic of desperation was needed to get our display underway too, unwrapping the patchwork, assembling it for the judges, and then getting it on display for the exhibition; and, most important of all, finally returning all these precious, much-loved, irreplaceable items safely to their owners. The job had to be fitted into the routine of a work-day already filled to bursting point.

Fortunately the magic, or rather the hard work of all concerned, worked, and the exhibition was acclaimed as the biggest collection of patchwork in the world, attracting an enormous number of visitors from all over Britain and from overseas. 'Many new enthusiasts for patchwork must have been recruited by the exhibition', wrote *Embroidery* magazine, journal of the Embroiderers' Guild.

* The Women's Institute (WI) is approximately similar to Women's National Farm and Garden Association in America.

The biggest collection of patch-work in the world. On display in the windows of Sanderson, London.

Patchwork exhibition. The large hexagonal patchwork on the wall is a Victorian table-cloth edged with lace. It is all worked in coloured silks with a black background. Some of the diamond-shaped patches are decorated with bead-work.

While also admitting 'that more ingenuity than skill or taste had gone into some items', the writer qualified this by saying that it perhaps came about in striving to be different. Not such a bad thing, obviously, as the article concluded by pointing out that the exhibition was 'an incentive to all patchworkers'.

That is what I want this book to be – an incentive to creative patchwork.

J. F.

Creative Patchwork

Anne Hathaway's bedstead.
Shakespeare's Anne had a crazy-
style patchwork coverlet on her bed
at Shottery, Stratford-upon-Avon.
Radio Times Hulton Picture Library

1 How it all began

The origins of patchwork, applied, 'crazy' and mosaic styles

'Patchwork should be, and was, the best use of the materials available, for our ancestresses surely had to use every scrap of everything they could, and not waste anything, and use their wit and ingenuity to make something useful and, if they could, attractive as well.'

That is not a quote from a well-known writer, but a simple fact stated by someone who has, as she puts it, 'a desire not to have the old homely purpose of patchwork lost and supplanted by sophistication'.

This is the tone of many of the letters I receive from patchwork enthusiasts. 'It serves as a sort of occupational therapy to me' . . . 'I took it up when I was ill' . . . 'it is so peaceful and relaxing, quite therapeutic'.

How did it all begin, this 'thing of shreds and patches', this oddity which makes something out of nothing, turning waste into beauty? It is something which perhaps more than any other form of needlework possesses a warm, almost human quality.

It is thought that the Crusaders going to Palestine in the eleventh century brought patchwork home to England in the form of gay banners. For centuries it was highly thought of at Court, and during the reign of Henry VIII fine specimens of combined embroidery and patchwork were made. It was really *patch upon patch* because before the motifs were *applied* to the foundation, they were elaborately embroidered in intricate designs; and even after that the edges were enriched with gold and silver cord. Thus *applied* work is where patches are sewn to the surface of the material so that they form a pattern either by their own shape and colour, or by the shape and colour of the ground materials.

Shakespeare's Anne Hathaway had a 'crazy'-style patchwork coverlet on her bedstead at Shottery, her cottage at Stratford-upon-Avon which you can still see there; it is made up of different sized patches, many of them long, uneven and straggly, but the whole thing is no less attractive because of the haphazard look.

According to the *Notes on Applied Work and Patchwork,* published by the Victoria and Albert Museum, London, the

13

vogue for *mosaic* patchwork (fragments of material seamed edge to edge), cannot be traced for more than the last two centuries in England.

'It would be gratifying to be able to follow its descent from the field of battle to the bedroom' says the writer, 'and could the existence of a single English patchwork quilt of the sixteenth or seventeenth centuries be proved, then an English ancestry might be claimed for the whole American group. But the fact remains that patchwork quilts do not seem to have been made in England until silks and printed cottons were common and cheap enough to be cut up before they were quite worn out. Thus from the end of the eighteenth century the fashion flourished, and all the poorer households had a quilt, patchwork on one side and plain, usually with the quilting stitches showing through, on the other'.

When thrifty Englishwomen went to America in the eighteenth century, they surely must have made up the best parts of worn-out garments into pieces for bedcovers. Padded coverlets were needed for warmth, even more in the New World than in their homeland, so many of the covers were quilted. The word quilt, incidentally, is derived from the Latin *culcita*, which means a stuffed sack, mattress or cushion. Obviously the stuffing (wool, flock or down) between the two thicknesses of material (wool, silk or linen) gave extra warmth.

The earliest known example of English patchwork is believed to be the patchwork at Levens Hall, near Kendal, Westmorland. It comprises a very large quilt and bed hangings made about 1708 from pieces of imported Indian prints, and can still be seen in the house. The work is composed of patches of five different shapes joined in a repetitive pattern. The bedspread is quilted with red thread in an all-over diamond pattern.

At the Victoria and Albert Museum is an English coverlet of the eighteenth century made up from fragments of silk and velvet. Many of these patches, squares and triangles have enchanting motifs – four-leaf clover, figure with parasol, animals and birds – embroidered in silver and gilt threads.

It is really extraordinary how many beautiful quilts were made by children in the nineteenth century. Observe the one made by a ten-year-old girl which is in the City Art Gallery, Manchester. From a variety of coloured dress prints she made an intricate pattern in patchwork and appliqué, concentrating on hearts and flowers. It should give you some ideas on what to do with your favourite old dresses!

Early patchwork. Made about 1708 at Levens Hall, Kendal, Westmorland where it can still be seen.
Mrs Bagot, Levens Hall

Patchwork quilt. Made of cotton dress prints with a series of borders surrounding a square centre patch inscribed 'Elizabeth Jefferson aged 10 years 1811'.
City Art Gallery, Manchester

Overleaf
Coverlet. English, eighteenth century. Made from fragments of embroidered silk and velvet. Note the unusual motifs in the triangular and square shaped patches.
Victoria and Albert Museum, London

15

2 Basic equipment and method

Fabrics – Templates – Papers –
Making and joining the patches –
Planning : Design and colour

It has been claimed that patchwork 'requires nothing that one does not have in the house already'. I suppose you could say that, because with some patchwork you would not need to buy templates, those small pieces of metal or plastic used to cut the papers accurately for the shapes needed to make planned patchwork.

What do you need as *basic equipment* to create patchwork?

Fabrics. The easiest ones to use are those that do not stretch or fray and which fold easily. Cottons, man-made fibres, silks and velvets will all do, providing they are non-stretch, non-fray and easy to fold.

It is best not to mix fabrics of different weights in the same piece of work, as obviously a heavy damask will drag down a fragile patch of cambric next to it. When mixing old and new, wash both – the new to prevent any shrinking, the old to make sure that it will take to water, unless the thing you are making is a decorative object that will not need washing.

Templates. In early patchwork the shapes were made without templates, those precise master-shapes from which the papers could be cut *accurately* into the shape required; materials were just cut and folded by hand. But quilting patterns needed templates to ensure the accurate repetition of an outline. Many old templates were made by the men of the family, from a variety of materials, usually oak, tin or card, with others in silver, brass, copper, pewter and occasionally ivory and bone.

Templates can still be made at home in the larger shapes; but as accuracy is so very important in the small shapes it is best to buy the commercial variety in metal or hard plastic. These are available in most of the traditional geometric shapes in a variety of sizes.

There are pairs of templates for each given shape and size, a 'solid' and a 'window'. The solid represents the size of the finished patch, and so becomes the pattern from which the paper linings are cut; the window is for marking out the actual patches on the fabric.

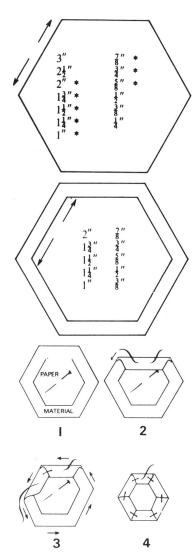

Templates (*top and centre*) Hexagon template; (*below*) method of using hexagon template.
Jem Templates

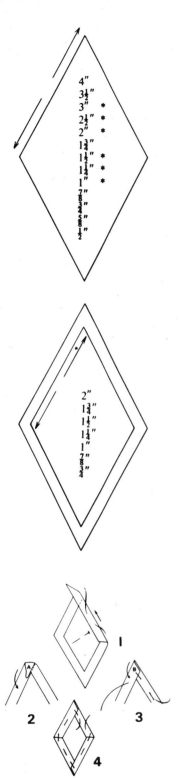

Diamond template sizes (top):
4"
3½" *
3"   *
2½" *
2"   *
1¾" *
1½"
1⅜" *
1¼" *
1"   *
⅞"
¾"
⅝"
½"

(centre):
2"
1¾"
1½"
1¼"
1"
⅞"
¾"

1

2   3

4

18

Needles. These should be as fine as the materials you are using, and sizes between 8 and 10 are best. Either 'sharps' or 'betweens' can be used; a 'crewel' needle, with a long eye, in size 9 or 10 is obviously easier to thread.

Pins. Fine and smooth ones should be the rule, to avoid marking the fabrics. Dressmaker's pins, brass lace-pins, and the very short, fine pins – 'lills' or 'lillikens' – are just right for tiny patches.

Scissors. Moderate in size and weight, but with good points and sharp. You need two pairs – one for cutting the paper patches, the other for cutting the fabric patches; you can use a craft knife for cutting the papers.

Thread. Cotton is suitable for most fabrics, but you need silk thread to work on silk. The cotton should be fine, 60, 80 or 100, and you can use it on linen, satin and velvet. When joining a light and a dark patch, the stitches will show less if you use a dark thread.

Bits and Bobs. A sharp lead 'B' (medium-soft) pencil, for marking out patches on the wrong side of the material. Use a white dressmaker's pencil if you have to mark on the right side of fabric. (Never use an indelible pencil or ball-point pen as they will mark the fabric.) A sharp razor blade or seam ripper is useful for any unpicking.

Paper. From which to cut the 'linings' over which the patches are constructed. These must be firm and crisp to achieve well-shaped patches and can be cut from good-quality scrap paper or card, (bank statements, company reports, if not too shiny, Christmas cards, and cartridge paper are suitable). You can buy ready-cut papers in various sizes too; the most important thing is that all the patterns for one piece of work should be cut from paper of the same thickness, otherwise the patches will not be identical. Iron-on Vilene is also suitable instead of paper where the material needs stiffening.

Michael Melia, who with his wife Jean runs Jem Patchwork Templates, recommends using a craft knife for cutting the papers. 'Cutting round the metal template makes for greater accuracy', insists Mr Melia, an engineer. 'Your paper is the most important step when starting patchwork and you cannot get such accuracy with the point of a scissor. With a craft knife you can cut several layers of paper at a time too.'

Making the Patches. The basic method is to cut out the fabric: either by laying a paper on the material and cutting a suitable amount of turning beyond it, usually about ¼ inch on normal fabric and a medium-sized patch; or by laying a template on, drawing round it (a coloured pencil is usually easier for the drawing) and then cutting along the pencil line.

The paper is put on the wrong side of the fabric and folded firmly over the material along one side, close against the edge of the paper. Using pale tacking cotton and a fine needle, the turning is tacked down with one stitch.

The next side is folded and tacked, pinching the turnings firmly into place at the corners. Continue all round the patch. To make sure it is folded accurately and with no gap left between paper and folded edge, another paper is laid on top of the patch, and if a very small amount sticks out evenly all round, the patch has been tacked accurately.

Joining the Patches. Two patches are laid together with the right sides face to face, and the papers outward, and fine oversewing stitches made along one side. The same depth of stitch should be maintained all the time and the stitches should be firm and fairly close, avoiding the paper. When the two patches are joined, the seam is opened and pressed flat, on the wrong side. It doesn't matter if the stitches are not wholly invisible, they are not meant to be – this is part of the characteristic look of patchwork.

It is best to sew patches into convenient groups or units, and for the units to be sewn together to complete the finished article.

Patchwork demonstrator Heather Ashcroft recommends her method of joining patches on the flat. In stitching a hexagon cover she proceeds with the work upside down, flat on the table, one hand underneath, slipping the needle through the edge of the patches. She finds that the stitches are invisible from the front and the papers are scarcely marked by the needle and so capable of more re-use.

Joining the patches. Heather Ashcroft shows a visitor to the Patchwork Exhibition (Miss Festival of London Stores) how to make patchwork.
Focus 4

Finishing off. When the whole area of patchwork has been sewn, all the tacking stitches are taken out, and the work pressed well on the right side according to the type of fabric that has been used. The papers come out last.

Pattern Design and Colour. There is no standard size for patchwork shapes: they can be as large or as small as the patchwork item requires. The six-sided *hexagon*, or honeycomb, is the easiest shape to construct, and can be arranged in a number of ways to create interesting mosaic patterns. The hexagon can be combined with the diamond and the square, to make other patterns; other shapes and designs will come to light as the book progresses.

Hexagon-shaped cushion. A design of wild roses makes a rose garland pattern on a plain ground – all of hexagons.
Kathleen Mecredy

Planning the Design. Planning falls into two main sections, Michael Melia claims: colour and the geometric shape, and use of the finished patches. He explains: 'In most cases one must look at the colour side first by deciding what material is available in terms of balance of colour, and then deciding on the size and shapes of templates you can use to give a proportionate pattern in relation to the size of the article being made.

It is important to remember that the more sides a template has the bigger the area covered by it, in relationship to the 'edge' size. So for a cushion a hexagon of up to 1 inch would be large enough; in the case of a diamond on its own you could comfortably use a $1\frac{1}{2}$ inch, and if one were using an octagon for a cushion, $\frac{3}{4}$ inch would be big enough.

Having decided the size and shape of your templates it is best to draw out your design on a piece of graph paper; and then using a very sharp pencil draw round your templates.'

A simple way to design is to arrange tacked, ready-to-sew patches on a cork mat or polystyrene (expanded foam) tile, playing around with them until a pattern emerges, formed by the different tones and colours. Then fix each patch to the background with a pin, removing the patches one at a time. To make sure that they are sewn together in the right order, make a rough drawing of the patches, marking the centre of each one with the appropriate colour.

A piece of *printed fabric* can be the starting point of a design; for instance, a small flower-patterned fabric with tiny rose-heads, could have the flowers cut out and centred in the patches and alternated with plain ones, the patches having, preferably, a common background colour, but the units (patches) must be carefully cut.

Colour Plan. Although colour in patchwork often depends on the fabrics you have available, schemes can be worked out. Try fabrics in several shades of one colour that have a different texture – but not different weight, because materials joined together should always be of similar weight since a heavy one could drag down a fragile one.

Combine colours – blues with grey, pinks with yellows, beiges and browns; gradually you will make your own experiments with colour, teaming vivid greens with bright blues, bright pink with hot orange, violet with green. The same proportions of two or more colours can be difficult to arrange into a good design. Try using varying amounts of each.

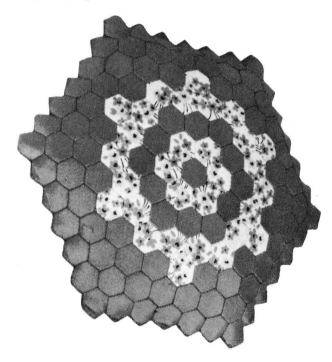

Hexagon-shaped pincushion.
Small floral patches form a rosette and circle design on a red ground.
Elsie M Gibbons

A dramatic effect can be achieved by adding a spot of rich vibrant colour to subdued shades but not too bright, or it will kill the delicacy of pale gentle shades. Experiments of this kind will show you something about the behaviour of colour; just changing the positions of light and dark patches can make an effective design.

Colour awareness can come from looking at simple, everyday things, the stained-glass windows in churches and cathedrals, the colours found in the hedges during country walks or bunch of flowers.

The beautiful colourings in a rectangular cushion designed by Doris Ross were inspired by walking by the sea. The background of plain greys and beiges were the pebbles; the delicate white and beige striped material came from the shells she saw and the reds came from flowers seen in a garden.

Mrs Ross says: 'The planning of *colour schemes* seems to be difficult for some beginners – mainly I think because they do not decide before they start where the finished article will be used. Why not use the colours of a picture which may be hanging in the room in which the cushion will be placed? A room with no pictures and which may have furnishings of green and blues suggests a stained-glass window where soft gold and reds may have been added to blues and greens, so some patchwork in this room using these colours would be most attractive.

'I used the theme *Another Day*, depicting dawn in soft yellows and the brightness of the day, sunset, twilight and night in appropriate colours. A happy piece of work!'

3 Patchwork shapes

Hexagons – Long hexagons (church window) – Diamond – Long diamond – Diamond box – Squares – Triangles – Octagon, Pentagon – Clamshell – Log cabin

Hexagons. It took Joan Bergh only seven months to complete her bedspread which won her first prize in the Women's Institute competition. She used over 1700 $\frac{5}{8}$-inch hexagons, producing a formal design of black, white, yellow, orange and grey diamond-shaped lozenges. This basic six-sided shape looks most effective when used in a dramatic, yet thoughtful way.

The patches were oversewn with around sixteen stitches to the inch. The background was a white, waffle-weave cotton and the outermost units of pattern were in black and white and yellow and white, with a ring in plain black. Within this area were units in an orange, red and yellow striped print, still with a black ring, and in a flowered cotton black on grey. The units of the central area were alternately a yellow and red print and a grey, red and turquoise print. The cover, finished with a black fringe, was very thoughtfully planned with carefully-chosen fabrics.

Hexagon bed spread. Beautifully planned design in black, white, yellow, orange and grey, the hexagon patches grouped together to make diamond-shaped lozenges.
(See page 26 for colour version.)
Joan Bergh

Mrs Bergh believes it is easier for beginners to work with $\frac{3}{4}$-inch to 1-inch hexagon patches, and her advice is always to press the work under a damp cloth before removing the papers. She does not recommend mixing silk and cotton.

Bridget Clarke's bedspread took over 1750 hexagons and two years to make, and she used a template with a plastic window; the wild silks and printed silks she used produced a colourful kaleidoscope of rich greens, blues, bright pinks and oranges, yellow, brown and beige, with the foil of a parchment coloured ground.

Miss Clarke feels it is vital that every patch should be cut on the same grain of material, especially when working with silk, as the light shows up any patches which are off the true.

Hexagon bed spread. Multi-coloured hexagons create a kaleido-scope effect on this silk spread. (*See page 25 for colour version.*) *Bridget Clarke*

Hexagon patchwork. Contemporary bedspread made of random patterned and coloured hexagons, bordered at the edge with half-hexagons in blue. Although there is no specific design, the effect is pleasing and colourful.

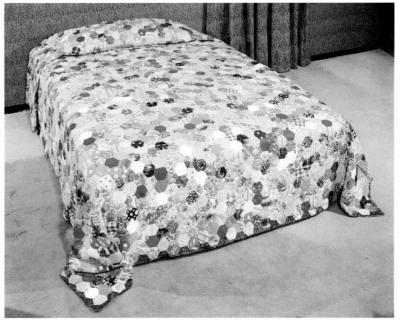

Hexagon patchwork bedspread. Colour used to interesting and dramatic effect in hexagons forming diamonds. Rich blues, greens and fuschia pinks combine with gentler shades on a neutral background. Blue patches make a clever 'interlacing' border.
Bridget Clark

Hexagon patchwork cot cover. Although the patches are not strong on design, there is a clever combination of colour with the pinks and browns on a parchment ground. Note the novel 'cross' patch effect on the cover.
Sheila Lonsdale

25

Hexagon and diamond spread.
Varying shades of green with salmon
pink form an unusual design.

Hexagon spread. Showing
variation of design on page 23,
when the spread is hung on a wall.

Hexagon cushion. A beautiful
example of well-blended colour and
design using small hexagon patches
to great effect. This enchanting
colour scheme was inspired by a
walk along the sea shore.
Doris Ross

Facing page :
Log cabin cushion. The light and
dark shades follow the pattern of
overlapping logs.
Joan Burley Smith

Friendship table cover. Contemporary patchwork 'autograph book'.
The patches are of felt, some embroidered with motifs and animals.
Doreen Masterson

Crazy patchwork. Victorian coffee-
pot cover, tea cosy, and egg cosies in
brightly-coloured velvet.
Author's collection

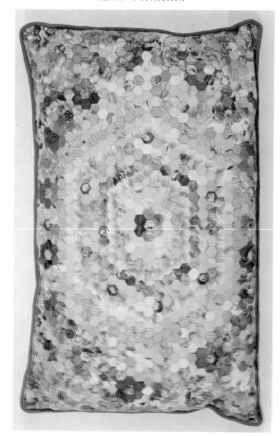

Applied patchwork. Contemporary
appliqué work. Diamonds, triangles,
hexagons and half-hexagons in
varied colours on a coffee-coloured
shantung ground contribute to a
magnificent kaleidoscope effect.
*Award-winning design WI/Sanderson
Competition worked by Norah
Stewart*

Patchwork picture. Contemporary
bird picture in silks using over fifty
templates.

28

Cot cover. Hexagons in pinks, fawns and browns are used to great effect. (*See page 25 for colour version.*) *Sheila Lonsdale*

Roughly 2035 hexagons were used by Sheila Lonsdale for a cot cover in pinks, fawns and browns in cotton, which took her a year to make. The cover is finished off with a covered cord round the edges, and she also found it was important to keep the weave of the materials all going one way. She advises a very careful selection of fabrics in the colours you want, right from the start, otherwise you find that you have made more patches than you need if the colours do not tone in.

Long hexagons, possibly so-called because of their resemblance to early English Gothic church windows, have been used to great effect by Norah Runham to make a bell-pull. There are

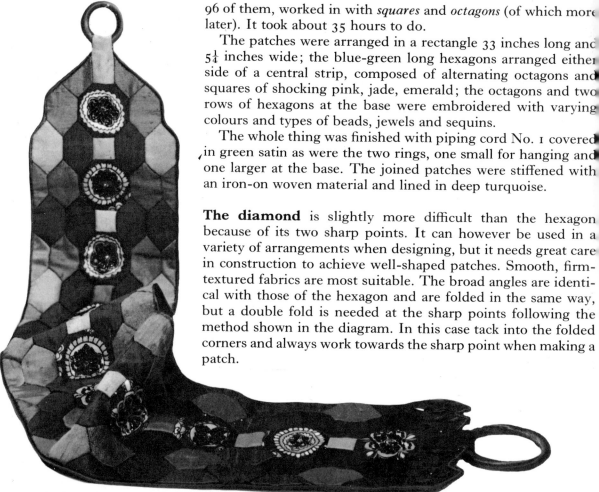

96 of them, worked in with *squares* and *octagons* (of which more later). It took about 35 hours to do.

The patches were arranged in a rectangle 33 inches long and 5¼ inches wide; the blue-green long hexagons arranged either side of a central strip, composed of alternating octagons and squares of shocking pink, jade, emerald; the octagons and two rows of hexagons at the base were embroidered with varying colours and types of beads, jewels and sequins.

The whole thing was finished with piping cord No. 1 covered in green satin as were the two rings, one small for hanging and one larger at the base. The joined patches were stiffened with an iron-on woven material and lined in deep turquoise.

The diamond is slightly more difficult than the hexagon because of its two sharp points. It can however be used in a variety of arrangements when designing, but it needs great care in construction to achieve well-shaped patches. Smooth, firm-textured fabrics are most suitable. The broad angles are identical with those of the hexagon and are folded in the same way, but a double fold is needed at the sharp points following the method shown in the diagram. In this case tack into the folded corners and always work towards the sharp point when making a patch.

Bell pull. Long hexagons (church windows), octagons, and squares (these are trimmed with beads, jewels and sequins) are used for a long-forgotten Victorian aid to comfortable living.
Norah Runham

Pincushion. Copy of a Victorian pincushion using long diamonds made from cardboard templates.
Miriam Moore

Diamonds can be used to make other interesting shapes – *star, box, trellis* and *cube*. An English quilt, believed to have been made in the mid-nineteenth century, and now in the Newark Museum, New Jersey, is made from scraps of silk, velvet, satin and brocade, cut in diamonds of uniform size, producing a three-dimensional effect of stars and cubes.

The pieces are stitched over bits of printed paper which include an advertisement of a puppet show and parts of a railroad timetable giving the trains to Exeter!

Long diamond. Miriam Moore has copied an old Victorian pincushion in modern silks and Lurex in blues, pinks, mauves and gold. There are 60 ½-inch long diamond patches pierced with 500 ordinary pins and some glass-headed ones.

It took her about fifty hours to make, and she admits it is rather a difficult item for a beginner, because the templates (she used cardboard ones) must be very firm and exact in size. 'Be sure to leave a good turning if using modern fabrics as they can fray very badly' she warns.

Diamond mosaic quilt. From Devonshire, England, mid-nineteenth century. Cut in diamonds of silk, velvet, satin and brocade, to produce the effect of stars and cubes. *Newark Museum, New Jersey*

The diamond box pattern is made from three diamonds in dark, medium and light shades of many colours, joined into a hexagonal shape and giving an even greater three-dimensional effect of a cube.

The American Museum, Claverton, Bath, has a splendid quilt called *Tumbling Blocks*, measuring 105 inches by 104 inches, and the really remarkable three-dimensional design is a giant star of silk 'boxes' formed of two diamond-shaped striped, figured brocaded and plain silk pieces combined with black diamonds on a grey and pink striped ground.

It was made by a Quaker, Dr Sarah Rogers, one of the earliest women physicians in Philadelphia, Pennsylvania, and was awarded a silver label inscribed 'Premium to STM for Silk Quilt 10th No 1852', at the State Fair, Trenton, New Jersey.

The Embroiderers' Guild have a box-pattern quilt in a variety of vivid coloured and black silks, plain, damask and printed. The boxes have a star border and centre piece, and it was made by the Duchess of Teck and given to the Guild by HM Queen Mary.

Another striking box and diamond quilt is in the Newark Museum, New Jersey. Called *The Heavenly Steps*, it was made in the early years of the nineteenth century by a Devonshire bride-to-be. The quilt top was made from pieces of silk, satin

31

Tumbling blocks quilt. American. 1852. The pattern gives a three-dimensional effect.
American Museum, Claverton, Bath

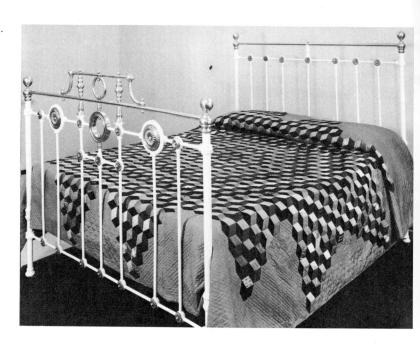

Box and diamond quilt. English. Nineteenth century. Made by the Duchess of Teck.
Embroiderers' Guild

and velvet, cut in diamond shapes, careful piecing being required to fit the corners exactly.

Unfortunately, the bride was never able to use her counterpane as her fiancé was seized for smuggling goods from France into England. In the Devonshire hills were excellent hiding places for contraband goods and the men who smuggled them. If caught, the man paid the penalty with death.

Box and diamond quilt. English. Early nineteenth century, called 'The Heavenly Steps' made of silk, satin and velvet. *Newark Museum, New Jersey*

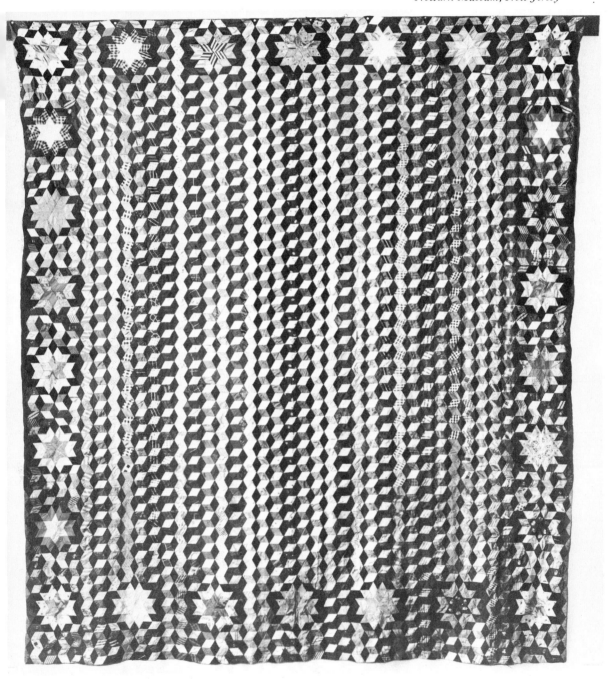

Square patch quilt. Staggered squares in a box design make a clever pattern.

Patchwork quilt. Composite hexagons made up of diamonds form the centre-piece with surrounding borders made up of squares and half-squares.

Squares. Quilts made from squares alone are rare. One cleverly patterned spread in the WI Exhibition incorporated staggered squares in a box design with the squares forming lozenges in the centre.

Another intricately designed quilt in the exhibition had a centre-piece of composite hexagons made up of diamonds, surrounded by borders of squares and half-squares, plus long strips forming the outer framework of the quilt. Doris Cook used square patches to make a patchwork sewing box, plus a tiny case for needles, thimble and scissors.

The making of a square patch needs a little extra care in order to produce a true shape. The final turning is the difficult part and it is a help to make this on a firm surface rather than in the hands. Doris Cook found that the accurate cutting of templates was particularly necessary to ensure corners fitting; very fine sewing, with small oversewing stitches as close as possible, is needed, with extreme care at the corners.

Triangles. An unusual coffee-pot cosy used 280 patches, mostly squares, diamonds and triangles. The triangle can be a half-diamond, or made by dividing a square diagonally.

Square patch sewing accessories.
The sewing outfit on the right – box, and cases for scissors, needles and thimble, has cerise red as the main colour, with lining and trimming of toning red and white floral motifs.
Doris Cook

Sylvia Murdoch ruled her design on cartridge paper first, then cut it out and used the drawn shapes as the template for each patch. Her colour plan was the careful use of sophisticated shades – turquoise, green-gold, and black and white prints. The plain patches highlighted the patterns and contrasting tones of light, medium and dark.

The octagon can never be used by itself. A square of the same size must be combined with it to fill the space that inevitably occurs. The regular *pentagon* will not make up into flat patchwork without the addition of another shape. A curved surface (such as in a ball) is obtained with the use of a pentagon – for instance 12 pentagons will make a ball, but if 20 hexagons are used with it a better curve and a larger ball results.

For a pretty, heart-shaped box June Cox used a variety of shapes most effectively – pentagon, hexagon, diamond, octagon, long diamond and square. The box was edged with cord and lace.

The clamshell patch is obviously based on the segment of a shell and its other names, shell, scallop and scale, are all appropriate because the scalloped lines usually overlap each other like the scales on a fish.

The usual method of construction is that an unlined patch is made by turning down the semi-circular edge only. This is done by fine pleating to make an accurate shape, following the outline of a card reproduction of the solid template which has been pinned into the right side of the patch.

Coffee-pot cosy. Mostly squares, triangles and diamonds in cotton prints and plains.
Sylvia Murdoch

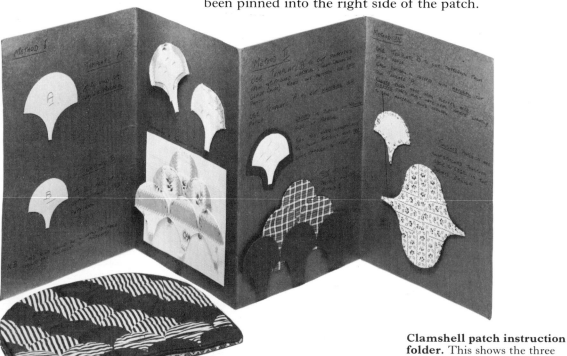

Clamshell patch instruction folder. This shows the three methods of making shell patchwork, and the finished article, a tea cosy.
Winifred Doran

Sweetheart box. Heart-shaped container incorporates a medley of shapes – pentagon, hexagon, diamond, octagon, long diamond and square.
June Cox

This card guide is unpinned as each patch is finished and used again. The patches are then assembled in straight rows – each row *overlapping* the preceding one by the width of turnings and making a continuous row of scallops.

There are actually several methods of making shell patchwork, which are illustrated in the teaching folder given to me by Winifred Doran. From left to right in the photograph see:

Method I. The large template (A) is used for cutting the material, and the smaller template (B), for cutting thin card patterns (the card used should be slightly pliable, about the thickness of a postcard).

The illustration shows the preparation of a shell patch and the setting up of a design on graph paper.

Method II. Use template (B) to cut patterns from stiffened material (canvas or glazed calico); then make one pattern for *each* patch. Use template (A) to cut the material for the patch. *Canvas* is placed on the wrong side of material. Turn the hem over the canvas and tack down. Stitches must *not* come through to front. Set up and proceed as for Method I.

Method III. Use template (B) to cut patterns from stiff paper. Each pattern is covered with *material* cut from template (A). *Convex* edges have hems pleated over. *Concave* edges must have hems nicked lightly to ease the material round corners.

Finished patches are slip-stitched together edge to edge in the desired design.

Patchwork demonstrator Dorothy Weir has developed a clamshell patchwork as a variant of one of the three methods described by Averil Colby in her book *Patchwork*. The finished effect has the 'neck' of the patch visible.

Each patch is treated exactly as all other shapes, tacked over the paper and oversewn together. The advantage is that an already-experienced patchworker is familiar with this technique and may find the unfamiliar hemming of unstiffened patches, as in the more usual style of clamshell, rather trying. Nevertheless, she points out that her method requires great accuracy and care in snipping the curves of the turnings.

A set of four bed curtains and valances in shell patchwork are in the Victoria and Albert Museum, London. The patches are made from a variety of dress prints and small-patterned furnishing prints, with groups of patches outlined in narrow green silk, hemmed on after the patchwork was made.

Alison Ferry made a beautiful shell quilt of 1664 pieces of glazed chintz over a period of some years.

Gold satin from her daughter's wedding dress was used by Kathleen Rickards for a charming clamshell tea cosy. Some patches placed with the selvedge, and others across the selvedge to give a shaded effect. This forms the design with the embroidery, for some patches have Tudor roses embroidered on them in stem stitch in green silk and decorated with pearls. The cosy is finished with a green piping cord, and has a cream lining and separate pad.

Mrs Rickards prevents the fraying of satin edges while working with just a *slight* touch of nail varnish round the raw edge. (Always test a scrap piece of the fabric first.) The piping cord was shrunk, and the material covering it used on the cross. The ends were tucked in at the sides into the lining; the bottom edge and lining were turned in and sewn together.

The log cabin is an evocative shape; narrow pieces of varying lengths are laid end to end representing the overlapping logs in the cabins of the early settlers. No template is necessary for log cabin as the patches are measured strips of material which are sorted into light and dark shades, with the strips worked into a square.

Every colonial home had at least one of these geometrically-arranged quilts, usually constructed from scraps of wool or cotton. A quilt made from scraps of silk, perhaps cut from dresses that were past wearing, was highly prized, to be used only for 'company best'. In the Delaware Valley and in Pennsylvania, log cabins were built by the Swedes and by German

Clamshell tea cosy. Made of gold satin, some of the patches embroidered with a Tudor rose and decorated with pearls.
Kathleen Rickards

Shell bed curtain. English. Late-
eighteenth century. The shell
patches are made of printed cottons.
Note the green silk outlining groups
of the patches.
Victoria and Albert Museum, London

immigrants familiar with the log houses of the Black Forest or of Switzerland. Isaac Weld of Dublin, who travelled through the country districts of Pennsylvania at the end of the eighteenth century, commented on the rough log cabins he encountered so naturally the log cabin is regarded as of Pennsylvania German origin.

A silk pieced quilt was made by Rebecca C Philbrook of Newark about 1906. The block, carefully shaded in light and dark, is made with a square centre, while four logs of graduated length are built up on each of its four sides.

A different placing of light and dark corners produced variations known as 'barn raising' and 'straight furrow'. A 'barn raising' made by Mrs Eliza B Riker in 1889 is entirely of plush, the wide garnet border being embroidered with roses, forget-me-nots, and daisies in natural-coloured silks. The heading and date at the top are also worked in embroidery silks. The practice of combining embroidery and piecework or appliqué seems to date from the 1840s. This piece has been mounted as a wall hanging, though the maker undoubtedly intended it as a counterpane. It was never a quilt, in the true sense, for it has no interlining and no quilting and is backed with silk.

A striking log cabin cushion has been made by Joan Burley Smith. The predominant colourings of the cotton strips range over light and dark shades of blues, reds, greens, lilacs, yellows and some white. Each patch is a square, but composed of strips of material. (See page 27 *top left*.)

Log cabin quilt. American. 1906. Silk quilt made by Rebecca C Philbrook of Newark. The narrow pieces of varying lengths of fabric laid end to end are comparable to the overlapping logs in the cabins of the early settlers. The patches are carefully shaded in light and dark. It is made with a square centre while four 'logs', graduated in length, are built up on its four sides.
Newark Museum, New Jersey

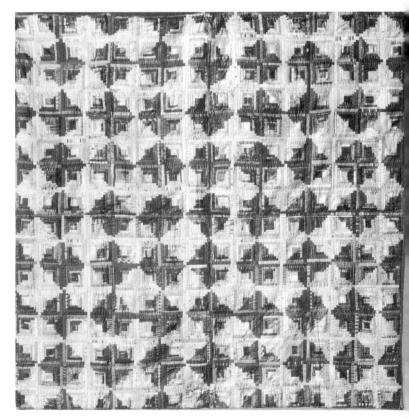

Pieced by Mother at the age of 71
1889

Barn-raising wall hanging. Made of plush by Mrs Eliza B Riker, 1889. Note how different this pattern is from the Log Cabin because of the arrangement of the shaded blocks in relation to each other. *Newark Museum, New Jersey*

4 Every patch tells a story

Patchwork with a history – Friendship quilts and quilting bees – Quilt names – Quilts from tie cuttings – Men and patchwork

To find out about old and unusual designs so that you can reproduce them, get inspiration to create something special for yourself, and perhaps form a collection of antique patchwork, you need to study the patchwork of the past.

Visit museums that include patchwork in their display of needlework, such as the Victoria and Albert, the Welsh Folk Museum near Cardiff, and the American Museum in Britain at Claverton Manor, Bath; in the USA, the Newark Museum, New Jersey, has a marvellous collection of quilts and counterpanes dating from 1680 to the turn of the twentieth century.

Sometimes the original paper patterns are still in the back of old patchwork, cut from newspapers whose advertisements often give an idea as to the date and place where it was made; old bills, letters and so on that were used for papers in the patches also provide clues for collectors.

A romantic, though rather tragic story goes with the patchwork bed hangings to be seen in the Stranger's Hall, Norwich. In 1782 Ann Margaretta Lloyd of Cardiganshire married her cousin John Brereton of Brinton Hall in Norfolk. Their first baby died, and in 1786 a second child was born, a boy, who became the apple of his mother's eye. While still a child he died from a fever, and for nearly a year his mother refused to be comforted. Eventually she was observed designing patterns from pieces of material and joining them together. She was making patchwork furnishings for her bed, and by the time it was finished she was almost cured of her grief. Obviously the patchwork had had a therapeutic effect.

The chintz patches, which included a passion-flower print, were longer than the long hexagon and appropriately called a 'coffin' shape.

A beautiful patchwork spread in my collection which has multi-coloured patches teamed with natural coloured ones, all hexagons, came with a letter telling in simple words this charming story of a 'Lady' who married a labourer.

Many years ago the first Lord Romney lived at Mote Park, Maidstone, and he had a female relative, probably a niece,

who fell in love with a choir boy at Willington Church which is in a corner of Mote Park, and she married the choir boy, a man named Tolhurst who was a farm labourer.

As an old man he worked for my father. His wife was an old lady when I was a child and was ill, and my mother used to help her and when she [Mrs Tolhurst] died she left the quilt as one of her heirlooms to my mother. It was said to be 100 years old then and made by women of Lord Romney's family, either his aunts or sisters.

This was mostly hearsay and the quilt came to my mother in about 1916, so it is difficult to fix a date for it.

The Tolhursts never had any children. If the quilt was made as a wedding present for Mrs Tolhurst it would be about 1860; if, as the story goes, it was old when she had it, it must be about 1815. Lord Romney's title is extinct now.

I bought another beautiful spread, quilted this time, from a retired farmer. It had been bought very cheaply by him in a sale at Eskdale, near his home in Holrook, Cumberland, many years ago. There can have been no doubt of their warmth-exuding qualities; three had been used as cow rugs, with only this one retained for a bed cover!

Hexagon spread. English, nineteenth century. Multi-coloured patches hold the romantic story of the lady who married a labourer. *Author's collection*

43

'Coffin' patch in bed hangings.
English, *c* 1801–4. Detail of the
valance made by Mrs John Brereton.
Stranger's Hall, Norwich

The exact date of the quilt is not known, but the unusual centre panel was printed from a polychrome wood block designed to commemorate the golden jubilee of George III in 1810. Cotton manufacturers printed these decorative panels from 1800 until about 1816. They were designed specially as ready-made centre panels to be sewn into the centre of a coverlet, and contemporary ones would surely be a marketable proposition today.

The quilt was probably made in stages, because on the corners are tiny medallions commemorating the golden jubilee of Queen Victoria in 1887, featuring the crowned head of the Monarch. The American equivalents were Presidential slogans printed on textiles which often found their way into patchwork.

A beautiful example which I have of *applied* patchwork (that is, pieces in the design cut out and *applied* to a plain ground) is a double spread in rich silks with velvet. Very fragile, the sides have been taken in to prevent the silk from splitting further. There is a silk fringe at the top and bottom.

On a broad border adjacent to the fringing are round patches circled with eight points formed from half-diamonds, their centres filled in with patches of velvet. These stars, and the richness of the colours (hardly dimmed by the years), give the spread an exotic Eastern effect.

It was made by a woman born in London in 1865 who went to finishing school in France. Her father was Henry Bishop, the owner of Gunters famous tea shop in Mayfair, London

45

Applied patchwork. English. Late-nineteenth century. Squares, half-diamonds and 'church windows' (long hexagons) in silk are applied together with large circles and hexagons of velvet to bands of silk: the vivid colourings are predominantly blue, pink, yellow and pale green.
Author's collection

(no longer in existence). With the coverlet the owner sent me a delightful letter written by the woman to her father when she was a young girl.

There is obviously plenty of patchwork still to be found in family collections which must have interesting stories hidden away among the patches. Some of the work in the Patchwork Exhibition, for instance, had taken years to complete. One, begun in 1908 when the owner was eight years old, was made from ragbag pieces collected from her family and neighbours in the little village of Shirburn, Oxfordshire; it was lined with the pages of her old school books, and she didn't finish it until she married, many years later.

Friendship quilts in the USA were signed and often dated on each block by the makers. These bedcovers, also known as presentation or album quilts, were made and given to a member of a community by friends to mark a special occasion, mainly around the 1850s.

Following a girl's engagement, some friend or, perhaps, her mother would arrange a 'Friendship Medley Surprise Party'.

Each guest brought her own materials for her block but the hostess provided material for the set. The guests had to work fast for no two blocks could be alike yet they had to be finished and set together before supper was served.

The girl for whom the Surprise Medley was given was obliged to return the compliment by asking the same guests to a *quilting bee* when her bedcover was ready for stitching.

Out of this idea grew the 'Freedom Quilt' in celebration of a boy's twenty-first birthday. The 'Album Quilt' might be regarded as the twin of the 'Friendship Quilt' since it, too, had individual blocks given by various friends.

A modern friendship patchwork has been made by Doreen Masterson, and she calls it 'a sort of sketch-book cum auto-graph book'. She began it a few years ago, and still adds to it. It incorporates multi-coloured embroidered motifs of personal and artistic interest, doodles and reminders to which friends add their own patches.

Intended as a table cover, it already has 217 hexagon shapes, cut free-hand without a template, and is made in coral, yellow and blue felt, using a fine needle and Terylene thread to work a herring-bone join stitch.

Each embroidered patch is framed with six plain patches, so that each one is clearly articulated. Many of the embroidered patches are in the nature of samplers, and it is believed that every stitch in the book is incorporated somewhere in the piece.

Quilting bee. American, nineteenth century. Even one of the cats is being lifted up to take an interest in the patchwork.
From a drawing by H W Pierce in the old-time New England Bulletin

Communal patchwork-making.
Made by members of Nottinghamshire Federation Women's Institute
for the 'Nottinghamshire' bedroom
at Denman College.
Worksop Guardian

Doreen Masterson told me: 'The patches serve as reminders of things and occasions which might otherwise have been forgotten – for example, a lobster celebrates a superb Lobster Thermidor I once enjoyed in Cornwall; an Aphelandra bloom fixes the one and only time it ever did! Cactus and a cow's skull remind me of a trip through the Mojave Desert; blackberry blossom of a lovely, if abortive, afternoon searching for blackberries in the Surrey woods when it was too early for them . . . and so on. (See colour illustration on page 27 *top right*.)

Finally, I do my best to encourage friends and relatives who may not have a clue about embroidery to do something with a patch on their own, with often quite charming results – such as a black flower with yellow leaves from a nine-year-old niece; a strange tree shedding its leaves shown on a patch I sent to Canada for a friend to embroider.'

There used to be communal quilt-making in the cottages and farmhouses of Britain in the nineteenth century, usually for a *marriage quilt*. A daughter in a family had to help quilt the coverlets to use on the beds in her home when she was married. She had to start at an early age, for the target was a baker's dozen (thirteen) for the wedding chest; the last one was the bride's quilt. An old Devon rhyme goes:

> *At your quilting maids, don't dally,*
> *Quilt quickly if you would marry,*
> *A maid who is quiltless at twenty-one*
> *Never shall greet her bridal sun!*

Working in groups is still done by Women's Institute members today. Members of the Nottinghamshire Federation of the WI recently made a patchwork quilt for the 'Nottinghamshire' bedroom at Denman College, Marsham, Oxfordshire.

The work was done in the traditional way, except that all the plain pieces have Vilene inside, instead of paper, and these remained in the finished work. The reason for this is that the plain material was slightly too thin and the Vilene has given it strength. After the work was completed the lining was attached to the coverlet by knotting.

The centre-piece is made up of nine blocks of printed material in oriental shades of apricot, green, brown and yellow, set off with plain pieces in yellow.

The template is a $1\frac{1}{4}$-inch hexagon and each block has 19 hexagons. Over 1000 hexagons were used in all. The printed material was cut so that each block formed a special design and the whole piece is set off by a border of brown. It is in printed blocks of three hexagons surrounded by a wavy line of brown. The background is green and the edge of the quilt has a double row of brown patches all round.

The plain background is a soft green to tone with the carpet in the bedroom. The four corner-pieces on the bed match the centre block. The border, which is 12 inches in depth, will hang over a valance of plain apricot, the same material as the curtains

Patchwork quilt. American. Pattern named *The Delectable Mountains* from John Bunyan's *Pilgrim's Progress*. The 'saw tooth' pattern is considered to represent mountains.
Newark Museum, New Jersey

Tie-cuttings patchwork. Precisely planned patchwork using various colours, plain and figured patches, all designed to form a complete pattern throughout. Shapes used are hexagons, diamonds, triangles, half-hexagons, and a centre block also uses pentagons.

in the room. At the base of the bed on the border, the Nottinghamshire WI crest is featured on a block of 9 hexagons by Mrs G W Fisher of Shelford WI.

The quilt was designed by Mrs D A Rickards of Welbeck Abbey WI, with helpers from Welbeck Abbey, Warsop, Shireoaks and other WI's from south Nottinghamshire.

Quilt names. Many American designs had names evocative of the times. The pattern of *The Delectable Mountain* obviously had its inspiration in the lines from John Bunyan's *Pilgrim's Progress*: 'They went till they came to the Delectable Mountains . . . behold the gardens and orchards, the vineyards and fountains of water.'

'To the pilgrims who found peace and plenty on the shores of America this quilt name must have seemed vividly symbolic', says a writer in *Quilts and Counterpanes*, the Newark New Jersey Museum's informative patchwork catalogue; (this quilt is in the museum).

The 'saw-tooth' pattern is arranged with mathematical precision and is considered to represent mountains. The quilting design suggests clouds on distant rounded hills; the whole thing is red and white.

An enterprising patchmaker of today could devise designs evocative of the contemporary scene – the Olympic Games, trips to the moon, 'pop' festivals, and so on.

Quilts from tie cuttings. One woman wrote that her quilt was made by her father's sister for her trousseau over 100 years ago when she worked in a tie-maker's workroom in the City of London; so the patchwork was made completely of cuttings from ties. It was never finished because her sweetheart died when she was making it.

Most effective patchwork can be made from tie cuttings. A quilt of silk scraps from ties was made in 1952 by Kezia Gray, using approximately 2,950 patches, hexagons, diamonds and triangles which resulted in a fascinating medley of patterns.

Another effective 'tie quilt' was made from Middlesex County Cricket Club ties by Mrs John Buchanan when she was 7. Her daughter Netta Rheinberg designed it and their initials were embroidered in the left-hand corner: RIB and NR, 1968.

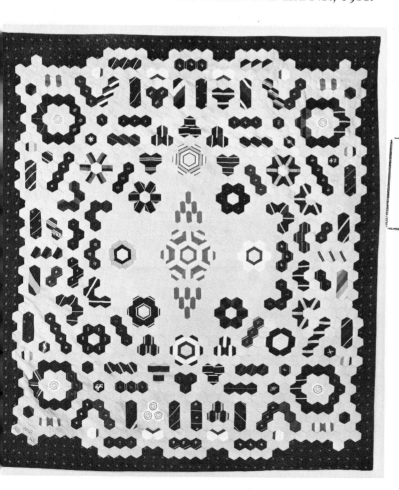

MCC tie-cuttings patchwork.
Carefully used hexagons, mingled with stripes form an effective design.
Mrs John Buchanan and Netta Rheinberg

Men and patchwork. Men made patchwork too. A painting by Thomas Wood *c* 1856, shows a Private Walker in the Fort Pitt Military Hospital sitting up in bed and sewing a patchwork coverlet.

A bedspread was made by a sailor, James Cox, in 1865, while serving in HMS *Victory*. He made it for his sister, Mary Cox who had brought him up, their mother having died when his sister was only 13, the grand-daughter of Mary Cox, Miss N Jefferis of Bitton, Gloucester, told me. The quilt is made from red, black and white felt-cloth diamonds, embroidered with flags.

James Cox, 1865 was serving in HMS *Victory* when he made a patchwork spread for his sister.

Felt diamond patchwork. A spread made by a sailor James Cox in 1865. In red, black and white felt diamonds.
Miss N Jefferis

5 'Crazy' patchwork

How to make it – Tea and coffee-pot covers – Quilts – Clothes

'Crazy' patchwork gets its name from the haphazard arrangement of the various pieces of brightly-coloured fabrics put together in crazy paving fashion; it is great fun to make, and easy too. The kaleidoscope effect was very popular with the Victorians, and is coming back into fashion again.

How do you create crazy patchwork? It is not necessary to plan a design, although sensible use should be made of the colours available when joining the patches. Each patch, which can be of different sizes (you do not need to use a template) has to be stitched to a backing fabric. This foundation can be of any strong material such as gingham, cotton or linen.

To make a simple 'runner' of crazy patchwork:

1 Cut your foundation to the shape and size of the article you want to make. Allow a good margin at the edges for turning. All the patches should be free from creases and with no ragged edges – so you will need an iron for pressing and the scissors for trimming.

2 Tack the first patch into place at the lower right-hand corner of the work, and as the material is tacked to the background, the edges of the patch should be turned under.

Every patch should at one point *overlap* the previous one. Tack each patch into place, covering the foundation material from side to side, continuing until all the foundation has been filled up.

3 After all the patches have been tacked on, the edges should be stitched with feather or chain stitch. When working these final stitches, begin sewing with the last patch tacked on the background, and work in reverse order to the sequence of tacking.

Use these instructions as a basic guide to what you want to make. You can use your crazy patches for a tea cosy, coffee-pot cover and egg cosies. These items were a great favourite with Victorian women. Some in my collection are made from brightly-coloured pieces of velvet. To make sure which was the cover for the tea pot a big 'T' was stitched on, and a clock-face, complete with hands and numbers of the hours. (See page 27.)

For quilt ideas look at the photographs of the two crazy quilts.

Patchwork quilt. English, nineteenth century. Crazy patchwork dated 1886 in the centre patch, and initialled MJR and CR in the corners. The pieces of coloured velvets and other materials are worked together with fine over-stitching, and the patches are decorated with flowers, birds and other motifs, and there is a grey velvet border.
Sotheby's, Belgravia

Patchwork quilt. Crazy pattern with blue border worked with embroidered yellow thread. Green, sateen-lined frilled edge. One corner marked C J Jenkins Rhoose × 1895, the name of the owner. The quilt was probably made earlier, as it was worked by the owner's mother Mrs Ann Jenkins.
Welsh Folk Museum

Crazy patchwork. Kimono in brightly-coloured triangular shapes. Note the wide sleeves and unusual round pockets.
Mrs A P Mitchell

Crazy patchwork. A turn-of-the-century crazy-style smoking jacket which could still be worn today. It is unlined, and made in numerous different pieces of taffeta with a plain edging.
Derek and Ursula Powell Antiques

The larger one, dated 1886, was sold recently in the auction rooms of Sotheby's, Belgravia (London), and the smaller one of 1895 is in the National Museum of Wales.

A simple crazy patchwork jacket can be made by feather stitching differently-shaped pieces of multi-coloured taffeta together, and edging with a plain band of fabric, using an existing jacket as a pattern. The one illustrated was made at the turn of the century as a smoking jacket, and is unlined.

A more sophisticated kimono can have brightly-coloured, triangular shapes arranged and tacked in position on a ground fabric. Again, the shapes are sewn with feather stitch.

6 Applied patchwork

Appliqué flowers, birds and beasts

Sewing patches onto a fabric ground appliqué or in applied fashion can contribute to really creative patchwork. Many of the applied patterns in traditional patchwork were cut from partly worn fabrics and stitched onto a new foundation in order to preserve them. Flower, figure and bird motifs were cut from printed cotton chintzes, which lend themselves to extremely interesting designs being formed.

In the Shelburne Museum in Vermont, USA, there is a coverlet with a very effective applied tree, bird and fruit design, worked in the eighteenth century. In the Victoria and Albert Museum another interesting coverlet, *c.* 1825, has baskets and sprays of flowers profusely applied to a plain ground. As Averil Colby says in *Patchwork Quilts*, 'It may not be within the capacity of every worker to design a coverlet of applied work as seen in this example from the early-nineteenth century, but today's cotton prints, equal to those from which these motifs were cut, are to be had for the choosing'.

A change of pace comes in another V&A confection from the mid-nineteenth century, where motifs cut in animal and figure shapes are used. With skilful cutting any of these ideas could be copied.

Applied panels of birds on a mosaic patchwork coverlet look absolutely stunning. I saw the coverlet, *British Birds* – an inspiration for all patchwork *aficionados* – at a display of Women's Institute craft work at Foyles Art Gallery, London, and thought it magnificent. Made by Dorothy Crampton it is also featured in the Colby book, and I can do no better than quote the description:

Bird motifs in earlier work generally were cut from printed patterns, but here appropriately coloured and patterned prints have been used for each part of the bird. A drawing or tracing of each motif was made and was then cut into sections – such as wings, tail, body and head – from which pieces of Vilene were cut out and covered with the appropriate materials, thus using the same kind of technique used in the eighteenth century. Each section is reassembled by applying it in

British Birds. Contemporary.
Applied bird panels set in hexagon
patchwork.
*Made by Dorothy Crampton,
featured in* Patchwork Quilts *by
Averil Colby*

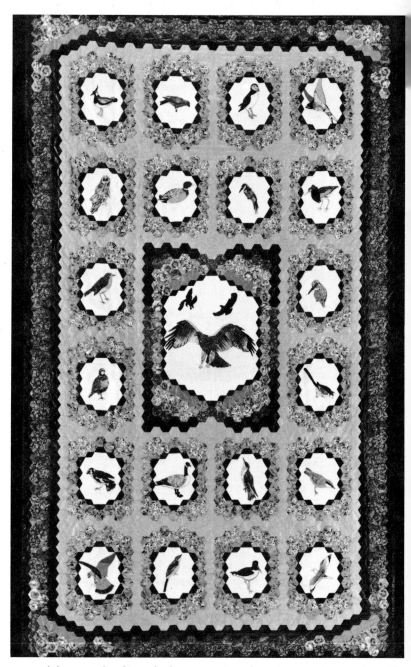

position on the foundation, overlapping the one beneath suffi-
ciently to be hemmed to it; wings usually are added last,
unless they are in a flying position.

Embroidery is used for fine details; beaks and legs are
worked in the appropriate colours, using long and short filling
stitches; eyes also are filled in according to the size and where
necessary; outlines – such as the white body of the Lapwing –
are worked in a single line of stem stitch. The crest of this bird
also is embroidered. The background of each panel is cream
linen, to which the birds are hemmed. Among those repre-
sented are the Lapwing or Green Plover, Puffin, Mallard,

Applied patchwork. Eighteenth century. Applied tree, bird and fruit design on a plain ground. An effective idea to copy.
Shelburne Museum, USA

Applied patchwork. *c* 1825. 'Cut-
out' chintz furnishing fabrics make
the applied floral motifs in this
pretty coverlet. Note the unusual
'Portugese' hem.
Victoria and Albert Museum, London

Opposite :

Applied patchwork. Mid-
nineteenth century. Multi-patterned
cottons are cut out in the shape of
figures, animals and trees, together
with familiar domestic objects,
(socks, shoes, glasses, bottles etc.),
and sewn on a plain ground. Try it
out for yourself.
Victoria and Albert Museum, London

Robin, Canada Goose, Green Woodpecker, Kestrel and Oyster-catcher; the centre panel contains Golden Eagles.

The patchwork is made from hexagon and diamond pieces in dress prints of dull pink and lilac on a blue-green ground, and others of predominantly dark bluish green. A single line of diamond patches surrounding each panel, and the covered piping cord with which the work is finished, are of dark green percale. The lining is unbleached cotton and carries the date and signature – *British Birds*. D M Crampton, 1959.

Norah Stewart made a most dramatic appliqué patchwork quilt which was runner-up in the WI competition. It took her several years to make, working mainly during winter evenings. She describes her work thus:

From metal templates I cut cardboard diamonds, triangles, hexagons and half-hexagons, then carried them out in plain and patterned dress silks.

I made a large central motif sixteen inches across, twenty-one motifs ten inches across and fifteen motifs six inches across. These I arranged and appliquéd onto a soft green silk shantung background. I made the centre more important with arranged single patches of wine-red satin diamonds and circles. I bordered the bedspread with an outer row of red satin diamonds and an inner border of colours tying up with colours from the centre motif.

I stitched the motifs on with a fine hemming stitch and then tacked it all on to a woollen backing and finally hand-quilted the background.

(See illustration at top of page 28.)

7 Patchwork pictures

Patchwork pictures – Inlaid and mosaic patchwork – Bird picture

Patchwork pictures are great fun, and some of the best are the work of a Mrs H R Harris who lived in a small cottage in Stratford, deep in the heart of Shakespeare's country. Many of these delightful pictures, worked around the 1870s, can still be seen in the foyer of the Shakespeare Memorial Theatre. Although they could perhaps be termed a form of fabric collage, Averil Colby, in an article in the *Embroidery* magazine rightly claimed them as patchwork in the true sense, in that the whole fabric in each is built by joining small pieces together in the traditional manner, any embroidery or applied work being put on to the patchwork foundation.

The Christmas Christening with the Holy Trinity Church interior shows the font in which the Bard himself was christened. All is faithfully reproduced in minute patches, including the detail of the stained-glass windows behind the font.

Another striking patchwork portrayal is the exterior of Williams, Glover's haberdashery shop, complete with half-timbered front (brown and beige square patches) with carving on the brown woodwork shown by chain stitch embroidery.

Other patchwork pictures, more on collage lines, were made more recently by Miss Elizabeth Allen, who was discovered and publicized as England's Grandmother Moses. Her pictures, which belong to the category of 'primitive' works, were exhibited at the Crane Kalman Gallery, London, when she was 82. Her ideas were fantasies of the East mixed in with the Arabian Nights fairy tales, and her own strong sense of morality.

Her pictures have a singularly period appearance, although many were made in this century. She used faded silks, shredded satins, worn suède, flannel, pieces of patterned fabric, beads and sequins, with blanket and chain stitches to outline some of the patches. In *Babylon Riding the Great Dragon*, thick lace is used to great effect; in *The Great Pyramid* coloured sequins make a glittering crown. Any of these ideas could act as inspiration.

Inlay work is appropriately described by Averil Colby in *Patchwork* as 'the connecting link between the true patchwork and appliqué. It has the construction of one and the pattern outlines

Patchwork picture. English, mid-nineteenth century. *The Christmas Christening* by Mrs R H Harris. The patchwork scene is of Holy Trinity Church Stratford-upon-Avon; the robe of the baby being held is a scrap of broderie anglaise, the skirt of the woman on the right is a piece of pillow ticking.
Shakespeare Memorial Theatre

Patchwork picture. English, mid-
nineteenth century. By Mrs R H
Harris. The half-timbered shop
front in Stratford is made of brown
and stone coloured patches.
Shakespeare Memorial Theatre

Patchwork Panel. 1851. Farmyard scene made from inlaid patchwork of scraps of felt embroidered in coloured silks.
Victoria and Albert Museum, London

of both, but it is more easily done in felted cloth as it is essential that the pieces do not fray'.

If you want to tackle this type of work Miss Colby recommends that the fitting pieces of the pattern can be tacked on to a *temporary* background of calico, linen or holland, but each must be cut with great precision, so that there are no spaces between them. The joining is often done by overcasting on the right side and the joins subsequently covered by a cord.

'It is important that the surface is perfectly smooth except for the overlaid cord where it is used. To thicken a thin material for use with a thick one, it may be lined with scrim or other suitable material before cutting out the pattern'. Another specimen of felt work is the bedcover made by a sailor that was referred to in chapter four.

Barbara Morris in *Victorian Embroidery* calls inlay work

'mosaic patchwork'. She cites as a typical example a farmyard setting of 1851, which is in the Victoria and Albert Museum. I think it is delightful, and scenes like this could be built up from scraps of felt.

Much more ambitious is the mosaic coverlet (also in the Victoria and Albert) divided into 61 separate panels with the Royal Coat of Arms in the centre. Episodes from the Old and New Testament are mingled with scenes of Wat Tyler and Robin Hood, while other notable figures are Shakespeare's Shylock, Queen Victoria and Prince Albert, Buonaparte, and Jenny Lind, the 'Swedish nightingale' of the Victorian stage. The poses of the theatrical figures are almost identical with the poses of the mid-Victorian 'tinsel' prints (literally pictures built up of glittering patches of paper and fabric, of which I wrote in *Collecting Georgian and Victorian Crafts*); the exaggerated stance had the characters with one knee bent and one leg straight, the figure lunging forward like a fencer completing a thrust.

To me this mosaic of different panels is closely allied to the friendship and autograph quilts already referred to, and a modern album of favourite characters could be built up in a spread or cloth.

A bird picture can be designed from pieces of silk. The one illustrated in colour (see page 28) uses patches of pink and green shaded silk overlapped for the feathers of the bird's speckled breast, while blues and greens form the striking plumage. The worker made her own templates, using over fifty patches in larger shapes with which she found it easy to work.

Patchwork bikini. Made of various coloured furnishing fabrics, and lined. In the bra the centre patch is darted slightly to fit under the curve of the bust; the edge has a piece of elastic running through it so that it clings snugly under the bosom. There is a hook and eye fastening at the back. The pants are elasticated at the top and in the leg.
Jean Amsden

Opposite:
Summer outfit. Patchwork hat in brown, orange and white diamond patches with silk lining, worn with the patchwork poncho, made from large hexagons and trimmed with a deep, black wool fringe. (Read about the footstool in the next chapter.) Hat *J. Dunn*; poncho *A. Watson-Gandy*

8 Patchwork fashion

Bikini, hat and sunshade – Skirt, jacket and waistcoat – Dressing-gown, smoking jacket and kimono – Apron and blouse

Patchwork from head to toe. Patchwork-covered umbrella; floor-length skirt and high-necked, long-sleeved jacket, both in hexagon patchwork.

A *bikini* in patchwork? Why not? Jean Amsden made hers in furnishing fabrics, 60 patches for the pants and 20 for the bra with the diamond shapes adapted to the shape of the garment. She made her own templates cut from cardboard, and the whole thing took her about three weeks, working about two hours a day. Her advice to beginners is: 'There are no short cuts in patchwork. Patches must be accurately cut, and properly tacked onto the papers; the stitches must be small and taken right into the corners, and the fastening on and off must be secure. If you are going to swim in the bikini, make sure the fabric is fade- and shrink-proof to withstand sea and sun!'

You can make a big floppy *sun-hat* in patchwork too, using brown, orange and white diamond patches, and a plain orange silk lining for the underside of the brim. Complete your holiday outfit with a snappy patchwork *poncho* in large multi-coloured hexagons, trimmed at the edges with a deep, shaggy, black wool fringe.

Don't forget your *sunshade*. You can cover a large umbrella inside and out with patches; or use the frame of a small Victorian parasol, edging the whole with dainty blue face. (See page 77.)

A glamorous floor-sweeping *skirt*, a sophisticated high-necked *jacket*, both look effective in brightly-coloured hexagons.

A man's *waistcoat*, in orange and cream furnishing fabrics, looks most dramatic, and should be a delight to any clothes-conscious male. Angela Dewar has made a very elegant waistcoat in 200 1-inch hexagons, forming a stripe, from Sanderson fabrics, rich damasks and silks. (See page 78 *top left*.)

Waistcoat. Overlapping clamshell effectively used to form this eye-catching design with scallop edge. *Rosemary Fountaine*

Man's Dressing gown. English, late-nineteenth century. Silk and chiné hexagons. Double-breasted, cuffed and collared.
Victoria and Albert Museum, London

Another attractive waistcoat, more a bolero, by Rosemary Fountaine, is worked with 100 1-inch overlapping clamshell patches. Flecked blue and white cotton poplin patches are most imaginatively teamed with groups of white pique 'shells' which have floral shells in the centre. Mrs Fountaine finds a cork mat most useful to plan designs on.

There is a patchwork *dressing gown*, probably a man's, in the Victoria and Albert Museum. Late-nineteenth century, the hexagons are of chiné and plain silks, the style double-breasted and buttoning to the neck, with long sleeves and shirt cuffs. It is worth copying, whether for him or her.

For more patchwork fashion, a late Victorian *smoking jacket* and contemporary *kimono*, look back at the 'crazy' patchwork chapter where there are two smart examples.

If you just want to bring a touch of fashion to small articles, try trimming an *apron* in patchwork circles at the waist and hem, and a sleeveless plain *blouse* at neck and waist. These patchwork touches will brighten the dullest garments.

Michael Melia has some useful advice in his booklet *Patchwork Made Perfect*. He suggests that you buy a simple pattern of the dress, skirt or trousers of which you like the style, lay it out on a table and see what size and shapes of templates would be most convenient to use. 'You may find that by interlocking the patches you can do away with some seams', he says, recommending poplin as the most suitable material for a beginner to use as it does not fray so much.

Patchwork apron and blouse.
Note the pretty patchwork circles at the waist and hem of the apron, and the hexagon shapes trimming the neck and waist of the plain white blouse.
National Federation of Women's Institutes Collection

9 Patchwork in décor

Bed covers, footstool, chair and seat covers – Cushions, lampshades and tablecloths

Patchwork in decoration looks fabulous – not only in the bedroom to cover the beds. Patchwork *spreads*, old and new, fit in with almost any décor; and footstools, chairs, cushions, lampshades, all have a million-dollar look when covered in patchwork. You need to be ingenious too, when you start to put patchwork on furniture.

Winifred Morton almost gave up the search for something solid to use as a base for a *footstool* to be covered in patchwork. Her husband went to their nearest industrial chemist and came back with a rodent killer container – empty of course! It was a rigid cardboard carton, circular and 14 inches wide.

This she covered in $\frac{1}{2}$-inch thick foam round the sides, increasing it to 4 inches on the top. The patchwork, made of 397 $\frac{7}{8}$-inch hexagons of furnishing satin off-cuts, was stretched over the foam.

Colourings are shades of blue and jade green with touches of lilac pink. The underside of the stool was covered with a piece of plain blue-green fabric.

Mrs Morton used the usual solid template to cut the papers and the window one for the material, tacking cotton thread for covering the papers, and Drima in dark blue-green for stitching the patches together in over sewing on the wrong side. It took her two months to do, working in her spare time.

Her tips for beginners are to press the material well on the reverse side with a hot iron before cutting, then place one side of the template parallel to the thread of the material. Leave all the papers in until the joining up of the patches is completed, to prevent the work getting crumpled, and remove the papers before putting the patchwork on to the foundation.

Period *chairs* look wonderful covered in patchwork. An old patchwork spread which was badly perished in parts had its good pieces rescued to dramatically and appropriately clothe a Victorian prie-dieu chair (which is, as its French name implies, a prayer chair on which one sat astride and rested one's elbows on the projections); and antique dining chairs take kindly to *seat covers* in patchwork; the one illustrated is from Averil Colby's *Patchwork*. Made around 1785, the materials used were

Patchwork quilt. This mid-
nineteenth-century French bedcover looks good on a brass bedstead against a floral wallpaper and
plain carpet.
Richard Bett

Patchwork quilt. Mid-nineteenth-century spread, probably French, goes well on a modern four-poster. Square patches of varying sizes form a striking pattern with strips of quilting.
Richard Bett

eighteenth-century wood block cotton prints. For contemporary seat covers make a pad of plastic foam and cover it in patchwork.

The rectangular *cushion* made by Doris Ross took 1,240 hexagon templates cut from old Christmas cards. She used white No 100 cotton and No 9 'between' needles. (See page 26.)

Patchwork cushions will give a lift to the dullest décor. 'Think out your colours and design first', says Mrs M Steventon, who made a delightful hexagon-shaped cushion in hexagon patches with a wheel-like pattern of tiny pink and white roses teamed with plain pink patches. She covers lots of patches and arranges them in groups, experimenting before sewing them together. 'Don't hurry, have patience and take care', is her advice to beginners.

Kathleen Mecredy's hexagonal cushion was her first effort, and is very pretty. Patches of wild roses form a garland with plain blue patches, all hexagons.

Half-hexagons and squares were used for Christine Hawkin's cushion in tan corduroy and black and white tweed, an unusual combination. She used 'ladder' and overcast stitching in mercerized cotton to match the colours, and it took her about five evenings to make.

Patchwork parasol. Victorian sunshade re-covered in brightly-coloured diamond patchwork edged with blue lace.

Miscellaneous cushions and covers. A variety of patches – (left top) seat pad in squares; (centre) cushion in hexagons; (right) pillow in three-dimensional 'cube' patches, teamed with (left bottom) appliqué cushion; (centre) seat pad in squares and triangles; (right) hexagon cushion.
National Federation of Women's Institutes Collection

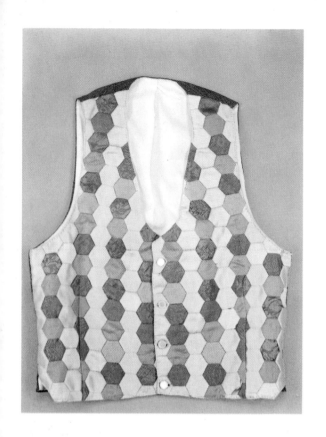

Pretty things. Triangles and squares make the box, squares the striped shopping bag; the little work box, pin cushion, needle cases and mat have attractive floral motifs.
Doris Marston

Facing page :
Man's waistcoat. In Sanderson silks – coffee, cream, orange and flecked orange; made of 200 1-inch hexagons which form a stripe. Lined in white, plain-backed and pearl buttoned.
Angela Dewar

Cushion. (Reverse of 84). Interlacing effect on a plain ground.
Doris Marston

Cushion. Squares, long diamonds, and long hexagons combine in this cushion.
Doris Marston

Lampshade. Long hexagons in brightly-coloured plains and patterns give a stained-glass effect when the light shines through.
Susannah Amoore

'Dora' doll pyjama case.
Diamond patches make the long-
sleeved dress and hat of this plump,
homely body.
Claire Richardson.
The three pig-tailed dolls and the
armchair were made by *Mrs W
Davies*

Irregular *geometric* shapes are a feature of Margaret Kirk-patrick's skilfully devised square cushion. She drew out 12-inch squares on graph paper, sub-divided into the irregular geometric shapes which were cut and used to tack material over.

To join the pieces they were oversewn on the back, using very small stitches, a very fine needle, and single-strand embroidery cotton.

Her sound advice for those starting out is: 'Don't be too ambitious with your first piece – attempt a small article rather than start something large, which would probably be cast aside half-finished. The main essential in patchwork, apart from neatness, is patience.'

Doris Marston, a well-known teacher of patchwork, who wrote the instructions for a template booklet, *Patchwork Made Perfect*, shows in one of her cushions how effective the combination of various shapes can look. She used squares, long diamonds, and long hexagons to great effect, with an interlacing of patches in the centre. The clever colour plan was pale and dark green, with dramatic touches of scarlet and white. The reverse of the cushion showed the interlacing patch effect again, on a scarlet ground. (See illustrations on page 78 *top left and bottom right*.)

Patchwork prie-dieu. Choosing a suitable covering for a prie-dieu, a French 'prayer chair', was a problem – not because of the unusual shape, but to retain its period look. An old patchwork bedcover that was badly perished in parts absolutely transformed a drab chair bought cheaply in a junk shop. It was not sacrilege to cut it up; it was a simple one-patch spread with no particular design.

Opposite:
Seat cover (one of a pair). *c* 1785.
Cotton prints with tiny rosettes.
Averil Colby

Cushion. Hexagon-shaped and
hexagon patches. A pretty combination of florals and plains in pink and
white.
M Steventon

Cushion. Woollen upholstery
fabric and corduroy velvet combine
to give rich textural interest, and a
mosiac effect.
Christine Hawkins

Lampshades in patchwork look most striking. When the light shines through the large drum-shaped shade covered in multi-coloured long hexagons by Susannah Amoore, it gives a rich, stained-glass effect. 'Most important of all with a lampshade is to use minute stitches', says Mrs Amoore, who used 40 Sylko and a size 8 needle. 'I had to stitch extremely closely because each patch had its edges clipped almost to the seam to give a clean-cut appearance. I also used a generous amount of plain patches to set off the patterned ones'. (See page 80 *bottom right*.)

There were no seams in the shade as just enough patchwork was made and joined in a circle to pull over the drum-shaped frame which had been covered in a stiff glass-fibre-type material.

Mrs P Edwards made a small shade in green and pink with approximately 130 $\frac{5}{8}$-inch hexagons plus some plain material used for the corners. The patches were made from plain and floral Sanderson curtain fabrics, cotton and cotton satins.

Panels of patchwork were backed by metal foil inside the lining to prevent seams showing when the lamp is lit. The plain panels of lined material did not have foil behind them so that light can shine through.

Patchwork *tablecloths* brighten up the most ordinary dining-table. They must have been used back in the eighteenth century too, as the Welsh Folk Museum has some hexagonal work catalogued as 'Patchwork tablecloth, 1780'.

A large piece of modern patchwork in gay colours is just right for the breakfast table. Make up a simple piece of patchwork in a one-patch design to enliven a dreary morning.

Patchwork spread used as table-cloth. Bright, gay 'one-patch' design will brighten up the dullest breakfast table.

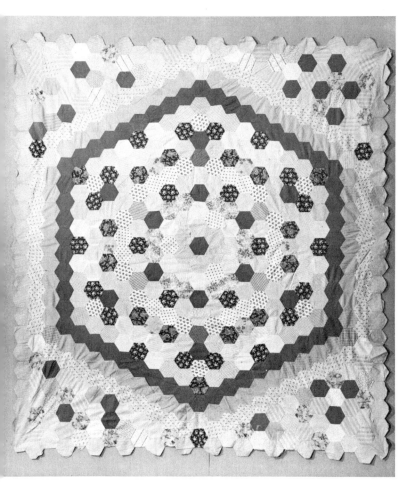

Tablecloth. Hexagon patches
c 1780.
Welsh Folk Museum

10 Patchwork playthings

Dolls and doll furnishings – Cat, ladybird and tortoise – Glove puppet

Four-poster bed. Miniature four-poster complete with bed clothes and curtains and patchwork bed cover.
Mrs P Yorke

Great fun can be had with patchwork playthings. A chubby 'Dora' *doll* can double as a pyjama case, and such cute pig-tailed creatures would delight any child. Claire Richardson used 110 floral diamonds for her mob-capped 'Dora' doll and strands of wool for her straggly hair. (See colour illustration page 80.)

'It is the most fascinating work', claimed Mrs W Davies, speaking of the rag dolls and the *easy chair* in patchwork she has made. She cut the papers from graph paper (1½-inch squares) more accurate than drawing, and allowed ¼-inch for turns, cutting out with pinking shears. Stab stitch was used to stop the papers slipping.

Cat. Masked feline creature in navy, green and white.
Phyllida Gaydon

Thin cardboard templates cut from old Christmas cards were used for the chair and left in to keep its shape. The chair was stuffed with kapok, rammed in with a pencil, the shaping made as it was done, to avoid lumpiness.

A miniature *four-poster bed* was made complete with bed clothes, curtains and patchwork bed cover; the curtains, bed cover and eiderdown were made in silk, mattress, sheet and pillow case in cotton, and flannel for the blankets. Hexagon patches, $\frac{1}{2}$-inch in size, 149 of them, were used for the tiny spread. The method of working was oversewing laid on a plain surround with feather stitching.

'A complete nonsense effort' is the description given to the masked cat made by Phyllida Gaydon. It's great fun though, in navy, green and white, made mostly in cotton with a little brocade and *broderie anglaise*. It took her 15 hours to make, using about 100 patches.

Maybe Lucy Ladybird and Toby Tortoise ought not to be in this book at all, because they are made from *pre-cut* felt shapes, but they are so delightful I could not bear to leave them out.

Glove puppet. Patchwork dress lavishly trimmed with rings, fringing, beads, and braids. *Ingrid Rowling, Embroiders' Guild Collection*

Lucy Ladybird and Toby Tortoise. Made from a variety of felt shapes, which can be bought ready-cut. Don't forget Lucy's antennae – blackened pipe cleaners curled round will do.
Jem Templates

Toby takes an enormous variety of shapes, $1\frac{1}{2}$-inch pentagons, hexagons and diamonds for his shell, 2-inch diamonds for his legs, $1\frac{1}{4}$-inch long hexagons and squares for the head, and $1\frac{1}{2}$-inch hexagons and diamonds for the base.

You can of course cut your own patches, using velvet and corduroy, but they must be turned over in the traditional manner so that they don't fray.

To design other toys, Michael Melia suggests first making up a mock-up in card shapes cut from a template and stuck together with adhesive tape; this way any mistake can be put right.

The *glove puppet* made by Ingrid Rowling comes complete with black needlecord hair covered in black bugle beads, with face, neck, and hands in natural shantung.

Coloured dress-linen patches were applied to a Viyella dress to form collar, cuffs, and hem. The colourings are blue, orange and mauve. The rich trimmings edging the collar are button-hole-stitched rings, macramé fringing and tassel-ended braids, some bead ornamented. The dress is lined with navy satin for easy movement.

11 Pretty things in patchwork

Boxes, blotter, notebook and magazine covers

Antique box. Lined with patch-work.
Valentine Browning

Boxes of all kinds look good covered or lined in patchwork. A pretty, antique *workbox* lined with patchwork looks most attractive. Valentine Browning used a glazed cotton chintz with a pale blue ground scattered with bunches of pink roses, and a plastic template to cut the material. She buys a piece of thick, clear plastic which can be cut with scissors, and makes her own templates. Papers of cigarette-card thickness are cut from a metal template. She applied the patchwork to a piece of the ground colour material and stuck it on card of the exact size of the *inside* of the box (curved lid, sides and base); this in its turn was then stuck to the inside of the box.

Alice Timmins covered a deep box most effectively in square patches, creating a novel effect with striped textures. The inside contains a patchwork needlecase and pincushion.

Square patches were used by Miss Lawson for a note-case and matching blotter, mixing plain and floral patches most successfully in chequer-board fashion.

Kathleen Barlow's *magazine cover* won its class in the Patchwork Competition. Carefully planned and beautifully made up, the delicate colourings of cream, yellow and green were quite enchanting, set off as they were by the bird motifs in the patterned patches (the fabrics were in fact off-cuts from some lampshade material).

Mrs Barlow works in the traditional way used by her grandmother. She uses good templates and windows when working with patterned material, and to get the pattern central she is very careful with her tacking, without sewing too close and so marking the material too much. Always use good-quality materials, she says, as it is a lot of work wasted if the fabrics don't last.

She oversews the patches together, working from right to left and so keeping the patches evenly together, with the left hand, working at the back with fronts placed together.

Pretty things in patchwork. A
work box in square patches incor-
porating textured patches by *Alice
Timmins*; a blotter and matching
note case by *Miss Lawson*; a
magazine cover by *Kathleen Barlow*

Further reading

American Quilts and Coverlets
Florence Peto
Max Parrish, 1949, and Chanticleer Press, New York

The Standard Book of Quilt Making and Collecting
Margaret Ickis
Constable, 1959, and Dover Publications, New York

One Hundred and One Patchwork Patterns
Ruby Short McKim
Constable, 1962, and Dover Publications, New York

Patchwork Quilts
Averil Colby
Batsford, 1965

Patchwork for Beginners
Anne Dyer
National Federation of Women's Institutes Booklet, 1969

Old Patchwork Quilts and The Women Who Made Them
Ruth E. Finley
Bell, 1970, and Branford, Newton Center, Mass.

Fun with Appliqué and Patchwork
Ilse Strobl-Wohlschlager
Batsford, 1970, and Watson Guptill, New York, 1970

Patchwork
Averil Colby
Batsford, 1970, and Branford, Newton Center, Mass.

Appliqué
Evangeline Shears and Diantha Fielding
Pitman, 1972, and Pan Books, 1974

List of Suppliers

Britain

Templates

Jem Patchwork Templates, Forge House, 18 St Helen's Street, Cockermouth, Cumberland

Miscellaneous equipment :

The Needlewoman Shop, Regent Street, London W1

Index